Start Your Own Business

Presented at Mesa County Libraries - March 31st, 2021
by Aaron Brachfeld

for my Father, who gave me the joy of business

אתה פותח את היד ומספק את רצונותיה של כל יצור חי

שתחיה לראות את ילדי ילדיך

ISBN 9798706701185

In business you must do more than earn profit to prosper. This book simply and elegantly presents advanced economic principles side-by-side with step-by-step tools, explaining not only HOW to start your own business, but the WHY of the methodology prescribed to transform profit into long term prosperity.

Originally presented at the Mesa County Libraries as a public information course, Aaron Brachfeld is a certified business coach of the State of Colorado and volunteers at the Grand Junction Business Incubator. He also instructs business classes at Western Colorado Community College.

1. INTRODUCTION

To say that the goal of teaching, or learning, the necessary skills and knowledge to begin a business in a half hour is ambitious is a dramatic understatement. However, since boldness and courage are frequently the most fundamental attributes to success through enterprise, it is fitting that we should at least try.

Mesa County Libraries is offering this course, and within its collections are numerous books on the science of business. However, this collection is too great to read, even in many years. And the vast body of science that composes economics cannot be learned even through any single PhD program, let alone by the dozens of masters programs available at our universities. It can take a lifetime of experience to gain experiences required to understand what is learned. None of this should discourage you: rather it speaks to the immensity of the science and better explains why you may expect the goodwill of your colleagues in not only your own but all other industries.

In business, neither learning nor lifetimes of experience are ever hoarded, since it is by this experience and learning we understand the interests of any individual lie in the wellbeing of their community - quite as much as the community is dependent upon the wellbeing of every one of its individuals.

Therefore, I would say the enormity of what you have set out to learn should rather encourage you. The vast treasury of public knowledge and experience has been opened to you, and it will suffice to take from it what gems lie closest at hand. You may at your leisure thoroughly read the materials here at the library and seek the assistance of the experienced members of your industry, many of whom volunteer at the Grand Junction Business Incubator. Take the time to attend the Western Colorado Community College, as well as our other colleges and universities, and talk to their masters students, instructors and professors for specific assistance.

No matter how humble its area of service, it is by your business that the purpose of our shared civilization is accomplished. Indeed, this is the first lesson I will teach you: for capitalism is not only the purpose but the means to our shared success, and the key to your prosperity.

2. THEORY OF CAPITALISM

As physics relies upon measurements of time and space, by dividing days into hours, compiling those hours into years, and measuring even the immense distance between stars in the humblest computations of inches or meters, and has created mechanisms by which to count seconds and standardize feet, so does the economist measure value through the use a ledger to register the flow of money.

Construct your ledger with columns organized in the following way.

DATE	JOURNAL	CATEGORY	INCOME	EXPENSE	BALANCE
This can also be used to measure other time (ex. hours)	This is a brief diary entry	Organize journal entries into categorical data, logging also tax deductions	For MONEY that is accepted, not merely earned	For MONEY that is expended, not merely owed	Income minuse expense plus previous balance

First, we begin with a column to measure time: we shall register events typically by business day, though some businesses (especially in retail) require registering events by the minute, or even second. It is by time we are later able to say if something significant occurred, and what the effect of that event was: many business owners will testify that before or after the pandemic occurred, business was very different. But others will direct their attention to cyclical events, like Black Friday, or even seasons, such as spring and fall. Some retail businesses must understand what times of day their customers shop. For restaurants, this is absolutely essential to success.

Every business owner should purpose themselves to understanding the secret knowledge of their industry's calendars: knowing when to plant and harvest, knowing when to change from summer to fall styles, when to advertise lawn services, when the holiday festivals truly begin and end. When is lunchtime, exactly? This is the fruit of experience, and its ripening is hastened by scientific observation.

But the date is also important to know for the sake of understanding the significance of current events as well: should the sunflowers have sprouted in our field? Should the shipment of supplies arrived by now? Should we plant again, should we order new supplies? Is it time to offer the pumpkin spices? Where is the evening customer rush? In fact there is no more fundamental data than the date; without it we are utterly lost.

Second in importance, we provide a space for journaling data. This diary of events provides non-quantitative data for us to understand what has happened. Whether describing observations which we should reflect upon later, such as when we first heard christmas music, or when we observed the last snow, we provide ourselves a reference for future years that allow us to anticipate fluctuations in demand and supply. This data provides context and meaning to the date.

Next, we look to categorize non-quantative data. The Internal Revenue Service provides numerous such categories for the use of deductions at tax time. Additionally, we may categorize sales to special clients, or purchases from selected vendors, we may carefully study the cost of gasoline over time, or the hours that we have relied upon our shift manager, or subtle shifts in the sales of particular products: does vitamin C sell better in the fall, or winter? Or spring? Better or worse than vitamin D? Has one of our clients reduced their demand lately? Or increased their demand? How can we better serve our customers? The business owner must understand what data is necessary to their industry. But no matter the industry, they will categorize that data using a ledger.

Fourth, we must account for our income - after categorizing and remarking upon it in our journal. This is because income is the purpose of our enterprise.

Fifth, we must account for our expenses, which are of fundamental importance as they relate to the costs of our income.

Sixth, we measure the balance of our income, minus the cost to obtain it.

Now, look closely! Here is revealed by our ledger a fact of immense value:

INCOME - EXPENSE = PROFIT

It would take a year of study to learn that income may be increased through the arts of MARKETING. And then, by another year of study, to learn that expenses are reduced through EFFICIENCY. And this prepares us to understand a profound fact: for it is by combining EFFICIENCY with MARKETING that we understand the costs of efficiency may exceed the benefits obtained by it, and that driving prices too high may cost us sales, and result in less profit.

It is only then we are able to understand the profound mystery that in seeking to reduce our expenses, that a NEGATIVE EXPENSE would increase profit: any time a negative is subtracted from a positive, it increases that positive value.

No, a negative expense is not hypothetical or imaginary. Understand it this way: a negative expense is that expense which purchases for us an asset. We call it "investment," for we in-vest our resources in this purchasing of capital.

ASSETS - LIABILITY = CAPITAL

When we understand not all expenses may be CAPITALIZED through the purchase of assets, we understand the success we desire lies within our grasp, if we will but reach and take it.

Consider, fuel is burnt and gone forever, but the truck we purchase to haul our lawnmower to the next city over allows us to reach wealthier clients, and dramatically improves our ability to market our services at a higher price, far beyond what that truck costs.

Understand this, and you will understand it is when we have capitalized all our expenses that our marketing potential has been reached, our business has matured.

Understand that, and you will be able to comprehend that in this maturity we have completed a lifecycle of business, and that there lies a greater cycle beyond that: when business is completed, the money we invested to purchasing its assets is never wasted, but from it springs new money: this is the origin of capital and the cause for wealth.

Therefore, we shall examine the phases in the cycle of growth, and develop our understanding of the science of economics into the philosophy of BUSINESS based upon an understanding of the business cycle, so we may understand when our business is completed.

3. A PHILOSOPHY OF BUSINESS

There is a limit to the amount of capital that may efficiently be purchased through investment. When we have achieved this full potential of our ownership, our investment is successful, our BUSINESS is completed: we say this because accumulating this capital was the philosophical purpose of our business.

There are three distinct phases our business is undertaken: a period of non-profit investment of capital, followed by profitable investment of that capital, and the realization of capital. This is a never ending cycle of growth: for that realized capital may then be reinvested.

What is this cycle of growth, and what is this *vita nuovo* of our completed business? What lies beyond the end of our work? At what point do we stop our investment of newly realized capital?

Imagine a dairy or beef operation:

NON PROFIT INVESTMENT. Without any profit, we first feed our calf, with milk from a bottle as we hold her in our arms. Eventually, she stands upon her own feet, and we continue to feed her, until she can eat her own hay. We still care for her then, keeping her warm at night, giving her medicine when she grows sick. We have invested her with our resources with no profit. But not without hope for profit: nor, indeed, without earning an asset, without earning capital. The investment is not yet realized.

PROFITABLE INVESTMENT. After years, after all this non-profit investment, she gives us her milk and we begin to earn profit.   We are enjoying profit in the form of milk: because of the potential for more profit, and the potential capital to be realized, we are incentivized to invest this profit further. Consequently, we still feed and care for her, investing her with more of our resources.

REALIZATION. Eventually, she gives us calves. These calves are the realization of all the investment of food, shelter, and medicine: from the first meal we gave her, we were feeding these new calves. And their calves too. And all their calves as well. When she no longer produces milk, or calves, our business is completed, and she gives us her life as beef: no longer in the dairy business, we turn to the business of butchering. Which, also, has those three distinct phases.

In each phase, there is the risk that the capital will not be realized: a calf could get sick and die, or even the mature cow could fail to fully realize the total number of calves she is potentially able to produce.

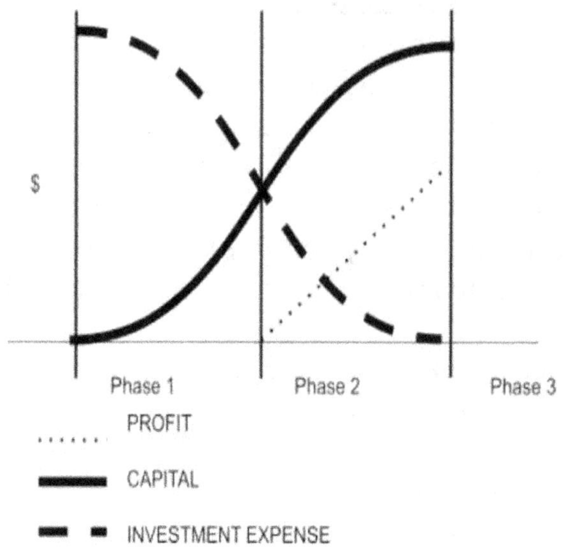

Examples of Phase 1:

- Providing food, medicine and shelter to a calf: the calf produces nothing saleable. This is non-profit benevolence.
- New employee hire / training: the employee does not meet quality standards. This is non-profit education.

Examples of Phase 2:

- Calf produces milk and calves, still requires investment of food, shelter, medicine
- Employee gains basic competence, still requires training, continuing education

Examples of Phase 3:

- Cow butchered: pure profit, all capital realized
- Employee no longer requires training or supervision, can train others

The cost of a calf therefore may be reckoned by the value of all the feed and care that went into its mother, and all of its mother's mothers, minus the unrealized risk that the calves will fail to mature to produce new calves.

Notice the calf will (almost nearly) always have positive value. This reflects the fact that within each calf is unrealized capital: the potential value of the calf, and all her future calves, minus the cost of the feed and care of that calf, and the calf's mother, and the calf's mother's mother, etc., even adjusted against the risk that the calf will fail to mature, is nearly infinite. For, theoretically, within each calf lies untold future generations of cattle, entire herds of cattle are unborn within the womb of each baby cow.

In this way, the wealth of our cattle increases to keep pace or even grow beyond our needs: each generation of cattle may become larger than the last (for even if we exhaust our pasture, we may by our profit purchase hay), keeping up or even outpacing the increase of our own children, and children's children.

In a simpler example, living in the home our parents built, we need not fear the night and cold as they did, and may instead improve that home to be better: adding plumbing, or electricity, for example. While our parents may have needed to be concerned about insulation, we could turn our attention to decorating our walls with art.

So does each generation of investor ventures further beyond what previous generations might even imagine possible. Our great grandchildren, simply by the care of our children, will be able to care for their great grandchildren.

Of course, as with cattle, there are sometimes disasters, or even unforeseen malice, but it is the general rule that with each cycle of business, there is more capital to invest than in the last. It is in the same way that our investments into our society inevitably progress it, and our ability as a species to withstand misfortune increases through time.

Technology, like cattle, also benefits from investment: technology improves with every generation, more efficient, cheaper, and more powerful. Crossing vast wildernesses by foot incentives us to invest those hills with trails, and invest those trails with gravel to make them roads; upon these roads our sandals once left footprints, but those will certainly be trodden over by the horseshoes of our children - and later forgotten under the tire tracks of our grandchildren.

Today we delve deeper into the hearts of mountains than ever before possible to find metals that our ancestors could not work in their primitive forges; we find ourselves capable of manufacturing plastics from soybeans stronger and lighter than any alchemist or metallurgist could once conceive of. Deserts are greened, first by irrigation canals, and then by the science of genetic engineering. Vast cities have grown and sprawl beyond the horizon, with towers touching the sky, their glass facades glistening in the light of countless new days to come. We flex, and test our reach, and find we may touch the moon!

It has been shown that it is the rule and not the exception that every one of our resources tends to increase, instead of deplete, through business. And this prosperity, and philosophy and method of business, has a democratizing effect on our society as the benefits of our prosperity are by service and industry made affordable to every member of our civilization.

Thousands of years of stock market records bear out this fundamental truth and lend credence to this philosophy of business, which is one of basic optimism and hope. Our disasters and tragedies are merely temporary setbacks. The science of economics confirms beyond doubt that the world is beautiful, and kind. And the people who live in it are good.

Shakespeare remarked, how wondrous is humanity! Indeed, by service and industry we demonstrate our ingenuity and resourcefulness and may reasonably look to our children with confidence. Today, on every shore lie ports and markets where we find people very much like ourselves ready to contract and complete business - even despite sometimes dramatic differences in culture, government or religion.

So it is that we say that the cause for wealth, this cycle of investment, lends context and meaning to our work: for by this, we see the end, the purpose, to investment itself. We understand at what point we stop reinvesting our realized capital.

This point, simply stated, is when profits are unsatisfying.

Why ever could profit be unsatisfying? It is unsatisfying because it is insufficient to earn profit. It is insufficient to realize that profit, there is no satisfaction in capitalism.

Food suppresses hunger only a little while, the hunger remains: the desire, to eat enough to live, will necessarily evolve by dissatisfaction to become the desire to fill our stomachs with better tasting, more nutritious food.

This basic economic fact is proven by understanding there is a limited number of meals we can enjoy in this life: this makes each one more precious than the last. The fact that there is a limited number of days to our lives inspires a desire to not only be filled, of good food, but to enjoy dining upon that food in good company, among our family and friends. To make each day better than the last.

We are human. Therefore we hunger. We thirst. There is no satisfaction for us! And this is good. We cannot rest, but must work. We must go further. Always further and beyond. That is our beautiful human nature.

When we understand this, we begin the adventure of not for profit business: an endless phase of non profit investment. This is the purpose and end of our realized capital.

Game theory teaches human beings require wealth for happiness, we simply cannot be happy without prosperity: we require the certainty of our next meal only so that we may turn our minds from filling our stomachs to greater things. A development of our service into humanities, the development of our industry into craft.

So it is that by degrees, we learn to love and protect the homes of our grandparents, the lands of our ancestors, and cherish our families and tribe, not to retire within them and to enjoy their great company, but so we may return home to them after our journeys and share what we have gained by our travels. We take from our own homes, the best of our lands, the greatest thoughts of our people, to distant places out of a joy of business; it is the joy of trading and bargaining that makes our entire world one family, and unites every land by well travelled roads.

When we feed that calf, we are feeding her, and all her calves she will bear, and all those calves too. When we ourselves eat we are feeding every one of our unborn children, and the generations to come in some distant future. The milk we eat came from the mothers of our calf, as the hay came from the fields our grandparents planted. The truest value of capital is that it is as eternal as gold, eternal as our desire, beyond all calculation.

But here philosophy becomes esoteric. Some have even argued this inestimable value of capital makes the defense of cattle worth dying for, even that the acquisition of cattle worth killing for. Indeed, wars have been fought for cattle. And land. And gold. But this argument is blinded, those who argue for violence are shortsighted in their greed for profit. For though while we might win a cow, or a pasture, the destruction of a single blade of grass starves thousands of our great grandchildren's grandchildren's grandchildren, and gaining a friend, a partner, is worth more than all the cattle of any world to come. Therefore, it is better to share a meal with your friend, however small, or even break bread with your enemy, than to hoard your grain.

Sometimes this esotericism has been combined with theology. Some have looked at the long journey to market as a sacred pilgrimage, and the work of industry and commerce as sacred acts; indeed, many markets have been dedicated as temples. It is amazing that your products and services are going exactly where needed most, at a price they precisely may afford. Night to night, day to day, your small business advances our society.

None can speak to the veracity of this, but such a spiritual journey may yet be reflected in the ledgers. Take courage, if not from the friendly gods you serve, than by the fact that in your ledgers you will see no past day has held you back, nor can any future day hold you back. You may grow weary, but you will never fail if you persevere but a little longer.

Whether you have a landscaping company or a simple warehouse, whether you are a broker or courier, a farmer or miner, a landlord or the owner of a taxi, whether you are a drop shipper or a retailer of luxury cosmetics, the host of a restaurant or a food cart, your small family business - no matter its industry - will have profound effects on you, and your family, and community. For generations to come. Each way of earning a living in this world is dear to those who practice it, for every industry and service is undertaken to live.

Life is short for all, every day dearer than the last. So make each day count. You have precious few of them. Never let your greed for profit make you lose sight of your place in this world. Rather, let it expand your vision, so you may see the true wealth, capital.

Studying prosperity, devoting ourselves to Prosperity, we may quicken the knowledge that wealth has never ever been conditioned upon resources into a profound wisdom of the nature of our world. When we understand wealth results from our labor we shall not only seek to acquire resources, but develop and then manage those limited resources profitably, and fully capitalize our expenses.

4. LABOR

Which brings us to the next lesson: the acquisition, development and management is the business of labor. Therefore, having spoken a little of its philosophy, I will teach you that proper leadership and organization such philosophy implies.

It is first important to understand a laborer is a sole proprietor who provides the service of labor. Therefore, we say LABOR is capitalizing service, that is to say that it is a service whose purchase, or expense, results in an asset.

When we obtain the service of a cashier to undertake customer service on our behalf, we capitalize that expense into a capacity to service more customers than we could alone. When we obtain the service of a harvester to pick apples on our behalf, we capitalize that expense into the collection of more apples than we otherwise might have on our own.

All labor is to one degree or another skilled or specialized, meaning that it required training, experience and other capitalization (such as licensure) to develop: the difference in quality of service provided, efficiency of service provided, and capacity to undertake that work arising from this training and experience and sometimes licensure is how we measure the value of that skill.

A skilled forklift operator may or may not have significantly greater value to a warehouser than an unskilled forklift operator, but certainly an experienced doctor will have greater value to a hospital than one who has just started practicing medicine.

But in every case, the doctor takes their skill with them from hospital to hospital, and the forklift operator takes their ability to drive a forklift from warehouse to warehouse, even if they do not own a forklift. This skill is their business, it is their asset. They own it. No one else can. And the freedom they enjoy to market their skills to where those skills are most demanded suggests the value we must place on labor's leadership and organization. For it is by leadership and organization that labor is made efficient, and the costs of labor driven down.

Therefore, while we cannot say that labor is the fundamental measure or elemental nature of wealth, we may say leadership is the method by which resources are converted by labor into wealth. And this is why we say labor is instead the atomic component of all business, that enterprise of investing resources derived by profit into assets required for capital.

And, by this understand that as we invest into labor by maintaining or retaining employees and developing either intentionally through training or unintentionally by experience, the expense in labor is capitalized.

We previously looked at the phases of investment, and saw they could be applied to the investment of labor with skill.

Now, understand: leadership is a form of labor too.

A business owner may provide their own labor, or require it in partnership, or contract for it through incorporation. But no matter how complex a corporate business becomes, it will always operate through the cohesion of individual laborers providing their own labor to each other through an act of transacting business through leadership.

Put another way, this cohesion that permits organization occurs through leadership. Leadership shapes the organization of labor so that it functions as a business.

5. LEADERSHIP: THE BUSINESS PLAN

There is no formal or "correct" format for a business plan.

Rather, its elements and composition are organized with the audience or purpose in mind. The process and methodology itself is designed to accomplish its goal.

Its primary purpose and audience is internal: communication, coordination and planning
Its secondary purpose is external: communication, to investors, and risk analysis

---

1. *Directives (products and services)*
2. *Executive plan (goals and objectives)*
    a. *Market research*
    b. *Demand-driven segmentation*
3. *Resource analysis (SWOT)*
4. *Resource management plan*
    a. *Maximize capital against limitations by efficiently servicing greatest demand value*
5. *Start up / operational plan*
6. *Legal analysis*
7. *Financial planning*
    a. *3 year cash flow scenario planning*
8. *Investor analysis*
    a. *Return On Investment (ROI)*
9. *Marketing plan*
10. *Efficiency (quality control) plan*

Leadership is undertaken through three kinds of actions: directive actions, executive actions, and management actions. Planning these actions is at the heart of the BUSINESS PLAN.

Recall that BUSINESS is the process by which we fully realize the potential capital of an investment. In this context, we may better understand that DIRECTORS represent the interests of these investors: the owners, stockholders, and stakeholders. Their directives, or guidance, direct or guide the business to this goal of fully realized potential capital. Typically, this is accomplished by describing the industry or service undertaken, the products and services offered, and developing a quantitative and qualitative measure of success, of this anticipated maturity, this potential capital.

Such directives require execution. This is accomplished by the EXECUTIVES. The Executives will develop operational strategies. This includes legal compliance, financial accountability, and of course the accomplishment of the various products and services.

The MANAGERS manage the limited resources of the business to accomplish the most of the more important priorities of the Executives.

Management begins by assessing those resources a company is STRONG in, WEAK in, those OPPORTUNITIES for marketing products and services and efficiencies in operations, and an assessment of THREATS to these operations. Strengths, Weaknesses, Opportunities and Threats analysis is commonly referred to as a "SWOT" analysis.

Marketing and efficiency will be discussed next. However, it is important at this point to notice that a proper management of resources determines the actions of the executives, and therefore must be guided, or directed, by the owners, stockholders and stakeholders: the Directors may want to undertake business as chef, but lacking the resources to acquire a traditional restaurant location, will guide the management of resources for the executives to accomplish the full potential of this business using non traditional retail venues, such as by the opening of a food cart, or by offering custom cooking services in the home kitchens of patrons. The operational assessment of the management determines what goals of the executives, as guided by the directors, are feasible, and which must be accomplished first: in this case, the goal of providing the service of food preparation, in the guidance of being a chef, is accomplished by management through a food cart or custom cooking services.

The resourcefulness and creativity of a manager in accomplishing the goals of an executive is therefore most important. This is best expressed in the practice of marketing and efficiency.

While there is no formal or correct business plan, and each business plan must be designed with the intended audience in mind - whether it is to be used for internal communication between the Directors, Executives and Management, or for potential investors or creditors, or others - it is a good idea to include these basic elements.

1. Directives
    a. A description of the products and services
2. Executive business description: Goals and objectives
    a. How will these products and services be fully capitalized
        i.   Description of how the products and services are used
        ii.   Description of their qualitative values
        iii. Who requires these uses? Who are the customers, clients or patrons?
        iv.   Develop these consumers into categorical data: analyze the consumers by what qualities are desired, this will reveal the demographical information.

For example, if some consumers desire vegetables primarily because they are tasty, but others want them primarily because they are nutritious, this reveals two categories of consumers. Analyzing the consumers will reveal commonalities: perhaps older consumers prefer taste, younger consumers prefer nutrition. This is useful for later marketing (showing the consumers how your vegetables are more tasty or more nutritious), but is also useful in understanding what products and services should be offered: if those consumers who prefer nutrition believe that spinach is more nutritious than cauliflower, this will guide product selection in accomplishing the directive of vegetable farming; if consumers who prefer taste enjoy broccoli more than radishes, this will guide product selection in accomplishing the directive of vegetable farming. It does no good to produce useless demographic information: to know that your average customer is 34 years old and female does not guide decision making as well as understanding why they demand your products and services, except to the extent that there are generational differences in communication.

    v.   Analysis determining the full potential demand for each product or service: include here information on how much each consumer would pay for the products and services. This information can be obtained sometimes by analyzing competitors and understanding what prices they are receiving for similar products and services, sometimes by experimenting with raising prices to determine price tolerances of the consumers.

3. Management's Resource analysis (SWOT)
4. Resource management plan: after analyzing the potential capacity given limited resources for each product and service (the supply), what goals are feasible, and which are most profitable given the potential demand and supply.
5. Executive start up and/or operational plan: how to enact the provision of these products and services.
6. Legal analysis: what licenses, certificates, land use zoning, and other laws must be complied with.
7. Financial plan: run a scenario with theoretical information to estimate cash flow and determine if the business will be profitable or even feasible given the amount of available investment. This is typically done with 12 month plans for the first year, 4 quarter plans for the second year, and 1 annual third year plan.
8. Estimated return or cost to investors for investors in 1, 2, 3 and 5 years.
9. Marketing Plan
10. Efficiency (Quality Control) Plan

6. MARKETING AND EFFICIENCY (QUALITY CONTROL) PLANS

MARKETING is the process by which products and services are provided at the highest potential price, by communicating to consumers how the business's products and services are most appropriate to their needs.

EFFICIENCY is the process by which the quality of these products and services are maintained at the least cost through QUALITY CONTROL.

The two plans, while distinct, do have significant overlap. The most important overlap is identifying which qualities of the product or service are most important to the consumer, and which are the most costly to maintain.

For example, if a consumer prefers the quality of tomatoes to never have more than 20% waste, but is unwilling to pay for the business to hire Quality Control engineers to ensure that each box of tomatoes delivered has no more than 20% waste, and is willing to accept even 50% spoilage, the efficiency and marketing plan will indicate that this is not a quality that is worth advertising or maintaining. If however, consumers will switch brands if there is more than 20% waste, the business must make plans to find ways to provide this quality, and also communicate this necessary quality to the consumers so they are better prepared to pay for it.

Marketing is undertaken in several ways, most important of which is the commercialization of quality. Quality is the business's primary product, it is their primary service. Consumers will not only pay for quality, but will maintain business relationships with the supplier of quality. There is always risk to the consumer in trying a new vendor, and though the devil that's known is always preferred to the devil that's not, it is a better strategy to not rely on this inertia and instead strive for consumer satisfaction so that it is not a choice of devils, but that trust and friendship emerge under a long history of "blue skies."

Such "blue sky" is an essential asset to any business, and worth investment.

Essential to this business reputation is the management of labor. Labor is initially unskilled, and only after years of training and supervision gains competency. It takes many years after that to develop expertise in skill. The management plan for labor must include supervised on the job training: the manager must develop a plan for lessons and skill building exercises designed to accomplish the standards of quality.

It helps to preselect labor with some basic skills: a competency test prior to employment to assess the professional skill of a laborer will allow the manager to understand where to begin their instruction and training. It will also allow the most qualified candidates to be selected: if a laborer lacks aptitude to either the skills they would apprentice, or the aptitude to learn and apprentice their master, they should be unconsidered for employment.

Loyalty of the laborers also will impact quality and efficiency: though with skill the number of mistakes and rate of successful operations increases, a disloyal employee will, through laziness, malice or negligence either damage the business's reputation through sabotage. Loyalty is ensured through a combination of both positive and negative pressure through incentives and disincentives. The greatest negative pressure an employer may place upon their employees is disincentivizing loss of the employment: if the pay, benefits and conditions of work are so far superior to competing places of employment, the laborer is generally speaking disincentivized against willful acts that would endanger their position. Positive incentivization, through praise and promotion, encourages the laborer to exert themselves.

In some companies, labor presents the greatest threat not only to quality, but to the business itself: employee theft, and other acts of sabotage, are expensive and so prevalent in the retail industry as to have become a byword. However, the costs of securing inventory against malicious employees is greater than proper incentivization methodology and in other retail businesses, laborers have been known to defend the company's assets against theft even to the endangerment of their lives. To incentivize a laborer to become willing to die for their company is not complicated, but does require skills typically lacking in those managers responsible for supervising and training the labor.

When markets are properly segmented by demand, by what they demand and why, and how they use your products and services, it is possible to target each demographic directly. Rather than take a "shotgun" approach and selling residential house cleaning and commercial janitorial services, separate websites or even separate DBA's can be made to specifically target each different consumer; indeed, a separate marketing campaign can be undertaken for house cleaning, house keeping, maid services, and assistive living services. Or even further, with specific marketing designed to appeal to women, or men, or consumers of a particular age.

The DBA's are nearly free to register under an umbrella company, as are distinct phone lines or emails that POP forward to a single email (if desired or needed). Distinct google maps listings can be made for each one to assist in passive marketing by search engine, or to facilitate distinct internet marketing campaigns. Presence can be claimed by opening UPS or FedEx boxes in different cities, lending the appearance of a more locally owned or operated company.

Marketing and quality control are themselves advanced subjects for study, requiring many years of study and practice to perfect. There is a great deal of creative craft in both: for quality control is about teasing information out of statistical data, and marketing is largely a commercial application of the liberal arts. A good statistician is as much an artist as a scientist, able to understand the nature of relevance (not only truth) by exploring data through their five senses, with acute and highly trained practices in intuitive, deductive, reductive and inductive logic and reasoning. A marketer is quite as much a scientist as an artist, able to understand the techniques required to achieve the practical emotive effects desired. Perhaps this explains why whatever brief introduction to marketing and quality control I may offer will be insufficient.

7. CONCLUSION

In beginning your own business it is extremely likely you will discover that there are many subjects which I have poorly developed, or did not explore with you at all. The intention of this course was to be an introduction, and it lies upon you to seek the assistance you require when, despite a cursory understanding of the principles and theories of business, you encounter a situation for which you are unprepared.

Indeed, this was the secondary purpose of my instruction today: to introduce to you the resources available to you as you undertake your business, that at every stage you may fully benefit from the knowledge and skills of more experienced business owners. As these resources were developed at length in the introduction, it only remains here to encourage you against those numerous deficiencies you doubtlessly now begin to observe in your own experience and abilities before you are overcome by doubt into idleness and despair.

The lesson of quality control is that good enough IS good enough. And in estimating the quality of your enterprise, do not hold yourself to too high a standard. Rather, take confidence in your basic competency, and your ability to grow and improve. Everything new is difficult, and it is because of this difficulty we find risk: yet this risk is the reason we ventured our capital in our business. Without risk, we find no profit to our work. Let this reward motivate you through those many difficult days ahead. I have no doubt that you will succeed, if you but have the tenacity and courage to try - for I have seen others succeed where you stand today, and with greater handicaps than you, lacking even a basic introduction to business or supportive resources. Not one dollar you shall spend will be wasted, for if it does not purchase your success at first, it at least has bought you a measure of wisdom.

Take pride in how we all place our hopes in you. You are worthy of our trust. And that we do depend upon the success of your great undertaking should not intimidate you. There is no reason to be overwhelmed by the work ahead: rather see that you can accomplish these many small tasks and feel your strength. As great as the difficulties that lie ahead, you are more than equal to them and they are more than worth the great rewards for your trouble. Therefore, be bold, act bravely, without hesitation, place your trust in good Fortune to recognize your devotion and begin!

Aaron Brachfeld
Grand Junction, Colorado
March 31st, 2021